FAIRS
AND CIRCUSES

MIRIAM MOSS

Topics

All the words that appear
in **bold** are explained in the
glossary on page 30.

First published in 1987 by
Wayland (Publishers) Limited
61 Western Road, Hove
East Sussex BN3 1JD, England

© Copyright 1987 Wayland (Publishers) Ltd

Phototypeset by
Kalligraphics Ltd, Redhill, Surrey
Printed in Belgium by
Casterman sa, Tournai

British Library Cataloguing in Publication Data
Moss, Miriam
  Circuses and fairs. – (Topics)
  1. Circus – History – Juvenile literature
  I. Title   II. Series
  791'.1   GV1801

  ISBN 0–85078–957–5

Contents

Fairs and Circuses of the Past

The word fair comes from the Latin word *feria* which means a holiday. Fairs have a very long history. The first Olympic Games held in Greece 2,500 years ago were probably part of a fair.

Long ago most shopping was done at markets. The first fairs were bigger and more lively markets. During the Middle Ages merchants came from all over Europe to trade at the

A cartoon showing actors entertaining the crowd at Bartholomew Fair.

Bartholomew Fair in London, Troyes Fair in France, the Nijni Novgorod Fair in Russia and the Leipzig Fair in Germany.

In between trading, merchants liked to relax and enjoy themselves. They were entertained by **miracle** and **mummers plays**, **morris dancers**, stiltwalkers and dancing bears. It was also a time for feasting. Stallholders sold 'fairings'. These were beer, hot chestnuts and gingerbread.

Another kind of trade fair was a hiring and mop fair. People carried signs showing what kind of work they were looking for.

When the River Thames in London froze over in the late seventeenth century, a special fair, called the Frost Fair, took place.

By the nineteenth century fairs had become meeting places, where people of all ages and backgrounds could be entertained.

Maids carried mops, shepherds carried crooks and woodcutters their axes. One special fair that took place when the River Thames in London froze over, was the Frost Fair. Crowds ran on to the ice to watch the entertainments or buy pieces of an ox that was being roasted in the middle of the river.

As towns and cities grew bigger, shopkeepers took over the trade that had gone on at fairs. By the eighteenth century the entertainments at fairs had become more important than the trading. Rope dancers, **conjurors** and **acrobats** showed their skills to the crowds. Puppet shows were put on alongside the swings and roundabouts. Mingling with the crowds were nimble pickpockets.

In the eighteenth and nineteenth centuries there were permanent fairs called Pleasure Gardens in European cities. There was the Prater in Venice and the Tivoli in

Copenhagen. Trade fairs did not die out completely, however. Billingsgate Market in London sells fish today and Covent Garden is still an important fruit and vegetable market.

The word circus means a ring in Latin. The first circuses took place in Roman times in **arenas**. The most famous arena was the Circus Maximus that could seat thousands of spectators. The entertainments were very bloodthirsty.

These people are enjoying some of the entertainments found at a fair. Children are riding on the carousel and playing on the swings, and some are eating cakes and sweets.

Roman chariot racing was a dangerous form of entertainment watched by many in the large, open arenas.

In the chariot races the charioteers tore around the course. There were some terrible accidents. Worse still were the gladiatorial games. **Gladiators** fought each other to the death. Sometimes gladiators used to fight wild animals captured in Africa. At other times giraffes, lions, elephants and rhinoceroses fought each other. Thousands were slaughtered in bloody fights.

The man thought to be the founder of the modern circus in 1768, was Sergeant-Major Astley.

He entertained crowds in London with his acrobatic horse riding. He soon added more acts, including clowns, and set up a permanent circus ring. Astley opened nineteen circuses all over Europe.

In 1793, John William Ricketts opened the first circus in America.

Sergeant-Major Astley entertained crowds in London with his acrobatic horse riding.

Later, Barnum and Bailey's American circus known as 'The Greatest Show on Earth' toured the world. It had three separate rings inside one tent and gave three performances to 15,000 or more spectators a day.

A nineteenth-century poster advertising the amazing Barnum and Bailey circus.

Humans on Show

During the Middle Ages, in the large cities of Europe, wandering showmen stood on busy street corners or at markets and fairs entertaining the crowds. There were all sorts of different entertainers. **Troubadors** travelled around with their own band of musicians singing ballads. **Mountebanks** put on free shows to attract a crowd and then tried to sell love potions and strange medicines.

The entertainers who were one day to end up as circus entertainers were called **jongleurs**. They often used pan pipes and a drum to draw a crowd, and at the end of their show they passed around a hat for money. The excited crowds watched puppet shows, magicians swallowing frogs, conjurors pulling animals from their hats, acrobats and **contortionists**.

Some entertainers thrilled their audience with dangerous and daring acts such as throwing knives at a human target.

Often a performance could end in disaster. These acrobats have fallen into a lion's cage. The girl on the left has been bitten on the arm.

There are many extraordinary and famous characters who have delighted spectators throughout the ages. There was a strong man who lifted horses and another who put a paving stone on his chest and invited the audience to break the stone with a huge hammer.

An American called 'Professor' Sands walked upside down on ceilings. He wore a pair of vacuum boots he had invented. Unfortunately he walked on an unsafe ceiling which collapsed and killed him.

One world famous trapeze artiste was Lulu. This daring girl turned out to be a young man! There was Zazel the human cannonball. He was shot out of a cannon into a safety net. Unfortunately one day he missed the net and spent two years in a plaster cast.

One famous tightrope walker called Blondin not only performed over a circus ring. He walked across the Niagara Falls on a wire 50 m (164 ft) above the foaming water. Then he trundled a barrow across, walked back again blindfolded, and then walked halfway across, made himself an omelette and ate it!

Another very famous entertainer was called Houdini. He was an **escapologist**. He escaped from

One of the most popular performances at any circus was the strong man.

The fireater's dangerous act has entertained crowds for centuries.

handcuffs, locks, chains, ropes and sealed boxes. He used to go to the police station and ask to be put in the strongest cell – then he would break out. He also had himself chained, put in a box and dropped in a river. He had to escape in four minutes otherwise he would drown.

Freaks and oddities were very popular in the nineteenth century. The crowds loved to stare at bearded ladies, the 'fattest man in the world' and even a man who had a terrible disease which made his nose look like an elephant's trunk.

An American called Phineas Barnum collected freaks. He claimed to have found a woman who was 161 years old. Then he sewed together the top half of a monkey and the bottom half of a fish. He called this the Fiji Mermaid. He also had a famous midget called Tom Thumb who rode in a coach 50 cm (20 in) high pulled by little Shetland ponies.

Two famous circus dwarfs, Tom Thumb and Minnie Warren on their wedding day

Clowns are perhaps the best loved of all circus entertainers. They have been famous throughout history. One called Yu Sze was the **jester** at the Imperial Court in China 4,000 years ago.

Today's clowns have taken their costumes from a theatre company that toured Italy in the Middle Ages. It was called the *Commedia dell'Arte*.

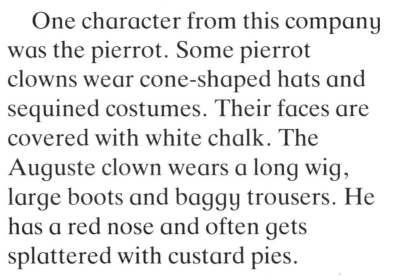

One character from this company was the pierrot. Some pierrot clowns wear cone-shaped hats and sequined costumes. Their faces are covered with white chalk. The Auguste clown wears a long wig, large boots and baggy trousers. He has a red nose and often gets splattered with custard pies.

The pierrot clown from the Commedia dell'Arte.

Children and adults love to watch the clowns at the circus.

Clowns can be world famous. One of the best known is Coco the Clown, who ran away from school in Russia when he was ten years old to join the circus. Life as part of a travelling circus is very unusual, as circus people never stay long in one place. They visit many countries living in large, well equipped caravans. They spend time between performances repairing equipment, making new costumes and practising their acts.

Animals on Show

For centuries people have enjoyed watching animals perform at fairs and circuses. In the Middle Ages travelling **menageries** appeared at fairs. Strange beasts, such as pelicans, hyenas and even performing fleas, attracted huge crowds. Astley's fixed ring circus started off by only using horses and dogs but soon he saw how popular animals were and added others.

Performing animals have always attracted a huge audience. These dogs are being trained to perform in a circus.

It is very dangerous working with lions, though they are a great favourite amongst audiences. This is a famous lion tamer, Neron, performing at the Paris Hippodrome.

The big cats such as lions, tigers, panthers and leopards, are great favourites today. It is very dangerous working with these animals. One famous lion tamer called Van Amburgh was appearing in America in 1846 with his gentle tigress, Edith. Suddenly she refused to obey him, and leapt at him tearing at his chest with her claws. At last someone passed a knife through the bars.

These elephants are thrilling the audience in Madison Square Garden, New York, USA.

Van Amburgh managed to stab her but died a few days later of **tetanus**.

One of Billy Smart's trainers was attacked by three lions and had to have 126 stitches. Now his wife stands outside the cage with a revolver loaded with blanks in case of trouble.

Elephants were first used by a man called Ducrow. In one act the trainer lies on his back and lets the elephant lower its foot until it almost touches his face. Any sudden noise could frighten the elephant into crushing its trainer.

Circus people are always looking for new attractions. Polar bears, sealions, **wallabies**, flying foxes and snakes have all been on show. In one daring act a man swam with six crocodiles in a huge glass tank. Bertram Mill's circus even put out a reward of £20,000 for anyone who brought them the Loch Ness Monster!

Many people nowadays don't like to see animals performing, or

Nowadays many people believe it is wrong to dress up animals like orang-utans and chimpanzees in clothes simply for the amusement of humans.

wild animals in captivity. They think it is wrong to make wild animals like chimps wear dresses or suits, or to make elephants wear hats and sit on stools. Because of this feeling people have tried to stage circuses without animals in them. Gerry Cottle started an animal-free circus but it lost him a

Many people do not like to see wild animals, like lions, kept in captivity.

quarter of a million pounds. The Circus Hassani, helped by the **RSPCA**, also failed.

People prefer to see animals in large, open spaces behaving naturally, so Billy Smart established the 20 hectare (50 acre) Windsor Safari Park.

Who is watching who? National game parks, like this one in Africa, allow animals to roam around in large, open spaces.

These mule deer are roaming free in their natural surroundings in a national park in New Mexico, USA.

More than 8 million people visit **safari parks** in Britain each year.

Other countries, such as South Africa, Australia and the USA, have large national parks where animals can roam free in their natural surroundings. And sea creatures can be seen in marine parks throughout the world.

Modern Fairs and Circuses

Circuses still tour the world today. One large, successful example is the Moscow State Circus. But other, smaller circuses are struggling to survive. The biggest single reason for these circuses failing is television. This gives people a much cheaper opportunity to see many first-class entertainers at home. There are still special trade fairs today. We can go to the World's Fair, Book Fairs, Motor and Boat

People travel for miles to ride on the exciting rollercoaster at a funfair.

A parade at Disneyland in Los Angeles, USA. The Seven Dwarfs wave to children as they walk by.

Shows, and Do-It-Yourself exhibitions.

Funfairs are now quite separate from trade fairs. There are still some travelling funfairs. But the fairgrounds that are on 'fixed' sites can have enormous, complicated rides which would be impossible to transport from town to town. People will travel miles to try out the exciting big dippers, the water splash and the octopus rides.

Two of the most famous fairgrounds in the world are in America: Disneyland and Disney

World. These have lifesize scenes and characters from many Walt Disney films, including Mickey Mouse and Snow White and the Seven Dwarfs. They also have many funfair rides and amusements. Disney World has separate areas called Fantasyland and Tomorrowland. In Europe you can visit Germany's Phantasialand Adventure Park in Cologne or Alton Towers in England.

Alton Towers is one of a growing number of permanent leisure parks, funfairs and theme parks that are being opened all over the world. There is a stunning array of rides, shows and an international circus. £5 million has been spent recently and most of it went on a new Grand Canyon Rapids Ride. It also has a corkscrew roller coaster and entertainments called 'Black Hole' and '1001 Nights'!

What do you think the first fairground attendants would say if

Mickey Mouse and friend pose for the camera at Disney World in Florida.

they saw a modern funfair? They were used to carousels that were roundabouts with chairs that were pushed around by hand. Instead of pop music they heard a noisy monster called a hurdy gurdy that could imitate every instrument in a brass band.

Soon after the penny farthing bike was invented, fairground attendants operated the velocipede. This was made up of many bikes joined together in a circle with the riders pushing themselves! The fairground attendants would

One of the spectacular funfair rides found at an amusement park in Germany.

recognize the dodgems which were invented in 1927, when everyone wanted to know what it was like to ride in a car. Now we are all curious about space exploration and we can go to the fair and ride in 'Moon Rockets' and play 'Space Invaders' in amusement arcades.

Fairs and circuses will no doubt change dramatically in years to come but they will always remain exciting places. Places where people can enjoy the feeling of being in a totally different world of mystery, imagination and colour.

Above *The fairground carousel remains a favourite with children.*

At night funfairs can look even more colourful and exciting.

Glossary

Acrobat A person who performs difficult gymnastic feats.

Arenas Places with seats round an open space where public contests or other spectacles take place.

Conjuror A person who uses magic to entertain people.

Contortionist A person who entertains by twisting his or her body into strange positions.

Escapologist A person who entertains by escaping from locks, chains and ropes.

Gladiator Prisoners of war or criminals and, later, trained men, who fought each other and animals in Roman times.

Jester A clown employed by a king or nobleman in the Middle Ages.

Menagerie A collection of wild animals kept for display.

Miracle play A play in the Middle Ages about the life of a saint or a Bible story.

Morris dancer A country dancer who wears bells on his feet, ankles and wrists.

Mountebanks People who sold medicines and potions in public places.

Mummers play A play acted out silently by masked performers.

Pickpockets Thieves who steal peoples' purses and wallets from their pockets.

RSPCA (Royal Society for the Prevention of the Cruelty to Animals) A society for the prevention of cruelty to animals.

Safari park An enclosed park in which wild animals are allowed to roam free in the open and can be viewed by the public in cars.

Tetanus A serious disease which harms the muscles.

Troubador A poet or singer of the Middle Ages, who travelled around giving performances.

Wallaby An animal that is similar to, but smaller than, a kangaroo.

Books to read

Circus by Elizabeth Cooper
  (Macdonald Educational, 1979)
Circuses through the Ages by Alan
  C. Jenkins (Chatto and Windus,
  1972)
Fairs and Circuses by Paul White
  (A&C Black, 1972)
Festivals and Celebrations by
  Roland Auguet (Collins, 1975)
Markets and Fairs by Jane Dorner
  (Wayland Publishers, 1973)

Picture Acknowledgements

Bruce Coleman 24, 27; Mary Evans Picture Library
4, 6, 7, 8, 9, 10, 11, 12, 13, 15, 16, 18, 19; Hutchison
Library 22; Wayland Picture Library 5; Zefa 14, 17,
20, 21, 23, 25, 26, 28 (both), 29.

Index